SMALL BURIED THINGS

SMALL BURIED THINGS

by debra marquart

american poetry series

© 2015 by Debra Marquart
First Edition
Library of Congress Control Number: 2013950948
ISBN: 978-0-89823-308-7
American Poetry Series

Cover and interior design by Sierra Fosness
Author photo by Richard Koenig

Small Buried Things edited by Thom Tammaro with Crystal Gibbons, Assistant Editor

The publication of *Small Buried Things* is made possible by the generous support of
The McKnight Foundation, the Dawson Family Endowment, Northern Lights Library
Network, and other contributors to New Rivers Press.

For copyright permission, please contact Frederick T. Courtright at 570-839-7477 or
permdude@eclipse.net.

New Rivers Press is a nonprofit literary press associated with
Minnesota State University Moorhead.

Alan Davis, Co-Director and Senior Editor
Suzzanne Kelley, Co-Director and Managing Editor
Wayne Gudmundson, Consultant
Allen Sheets, Art Director
Thom Tammaro, Poetry Editor
Kevin Carollo, MVP Poetry Coordinator

Publishing Interns:
David Binkard, Katelin Hansen, Jan Hough, Kjersti Maday, Daniel Shudlick,
Lauren Stanislawski, Michele F. Valenti

Small Buried Things Book Team:
Jan Hough, Lauren Johnson, Hannah Kiges, Jonah Volheim

Printed in the USA
New Rivers Press books are distributed by Small Press Distribution.

 New Rivers Press
c/o MSUM
1104 7th Avenue South
Moorhead, MN 56563

For Tom, Adam, and Gabe

CONTENTS

WILD THYME

THINGS NOT TO PUT IN YOUR MOUTH

— Medical Display, Iowa State Historical Museum, Des Moines, Iowa

a penny   a quarter   a button   a paperclip
  safety pins, closed and open
    most ingested while changing diapers

In two shadow boxes, Dr. James Downing displayed the objects
  he'd extracted from patients' food and air passages
    between 1929 and 1956.

a wishbone   a kernel of corn (overlarge)   a pen nib
  beads from a necklace with the string still attached
    a nail   a screw   a cover from a bottle of Anacin

Thumbtacked in rows, suspended in glassine envelopes
  the objects floated in glass cases, a warning
    about things not to put in your mouth.

a toothpick   a rhinestone earring   a wadded up ball of paper
  a metal snap   a cocklebur seed, spikey as a porcupine
    a long sewing needle   a sardine can turnkey

many small chicken bones   things with sharp edges
  cumbersome things that get caught in the throat
    things that go down hard and refuse to come up

a Daughters of the American Revolution pendant
  a gold hinge from a jewelry box   a price tag marked 89 cents
    for Item #1025293 from the Younkers Department Store

The exhibit includes the doctor's leather medical bag
  and his instruments of extraction   a tracheal dilator
    a uvula dilator   laryngeal and esophageal forceps

with a humorous note, jotted in a hospital report,
      "feed her anything but nickels and pennies"
            beside the nickel extracted from the child's throat.

GREYHOUND DAYS

KABLOOEY IS THE SOUND YOU'LL HEAR

then plaster falling and the billow of gypsum
after your sister blows a hole in the ceiling
of your brother's bedroom with the shotgun
he left loaded and resting on his dresser.

It's Saturday, and the men are in the fields.
You and your sister are cleaning house
with your mother. Maybe your sister hates
cleaning that much, or maybe she's just

that thorough, but somehow she has lifted
the gun to dust it or dust under it (you are busy
mopping the stairs) and from the top landing
where you stand, you turn toward the sound

to see your sister cradling the smoking shotgun
in her surprised arms, like a beauty queen
clutching a bouquet of long-stemmed roses
after being pronounced the official winner.

Then the smell of burnt gunpowder
reaches you, dirty orange and sulfurous,
like spent fireworks, and through the veil
of smoke you see a hole smoldering

above her head, a halo of perforations
in the ceiling—the drywall blown clean
through insulation to naked joists, that dark
constellation where the buckshot spread.

The look on your sister's face is pure
shitfaced shock. You'd like to stop and
photograph it for blackmail or future
family stories but now you must focus

on the face of your mother, frozen at the base
of the stairs where she has rushed from
vacuuming or waxing, her frantic eyes
searching your face for some clue

about the extent of the catastrophe
that's just visited. But it's like that heavy
quicksand dream where you can't move
or speak, so your mother scrambles up the steps

on all fours, rushes past you, to the room
where your sister has just now found her voice,
already screaming her story—*it just went off!
it just went off!*—as if a shotgun left to rest

on safety would rise and fire itself.
All this will be hashed and re-hashed around
the supper table, but what stays with you
all these years later, what you cannot forget,

is that moment when your mother
waited at the bottom of the steps
for a word from you, one word,
and all you could offer her was silence.

NEVER MIND

Lately, I've been forgetting the words for things.
Tortilla, for example, in the Mexican restaurant.
I am helpless. *A type of flatbread, made from wheat*

or corn, I offer description in the absence
of the right word or shout, *What is the casing*
in which a burrito is wrapped, as if this were *Jeopardy!*

Lately, too, I've been calling myself, surprised
to see my own name light up the phone display
when the landline part of me dials the cell,

lost in the tangle of sheets or left behind
the stack of books still mulling over something
I read by Pessoa. Never mind. My brain

cleans out its closets each night, discards words
and phrases like garments that are old-fashioned,
ill-fitting, or haven't been off their hangers in years.

"Can you help me out," my student says.
"What's the name of that tragic jazz singer?"
(She thinks I'll know this because I'm old.)

Voice like Chinese porcelain, gardenia behind
the ear. We puzzle over it for minutes
before I google, "lady sings the blues."

And then there's the strange case of my friend
the botanist, who can reel off the Latin name
of any plant—castor bean (*ricinus communis*),

black cohosh (*cimicifuga racemosa*), mugwort
(*artemisia vulgaris*)—but who could not remember
the title of a film or the actors who starred in it

if you tied her down and beat the bottoms
of her feet. "Lover Boy," is how she refers
to every movie star. "You know, the one

who was married to that Cutie-Pie." Surely,
this is medical. I must request the Latin name
for the remedy, or stop by the apothecary,

or just break down and visit my physician—
good old what's-her-name—and confess all.
Never mind. The phone is sure to ring someday

from the endless bottom of my purse.
The message, when I retrieve it, will be long
and full of unrecognizable jargon, the voice

of the nurse, no doubt, with all the gory details.

GREYHOUND DAYS

Because your mother is the Typhoid Mary
of travel. Because lightning, blizzards, locusts,
plague her travel days. Because that one time

in Minneapolis, some pilot-error, failing
engine part, or threat of nuclear disaster
necessitated an overnight stay, she now refuses

to fly. Too often, she will recount that night
for you—the cold shuttle ride to the hotel,
no PJs, toothbrush, clean undies, or sleep,

where all night she watched the green hinge
click of digits until the three a.m. wake-up call.
Besides, she says, why start out in Bismarck

going westbound for Bozeman by catching
an eastbound flight to Minneapolis?
So it's Greyhound days for her, and for you,

this day after Christmas, it's the drop-off drive
to the truck stop on the unlit edge of town,
where you'll stamp your feet, puff your cheeks

in the snowy dark, waiting for the Greyhound
with the Goth girls and the tattooed boys,
with the gaunt-cheeked, luggage-less

chain-smoker, and that one young mother
who's been criss-crossing the country
with her two toddlers and a colicky baby

since your own Greyhound days. You realize
at the approaching purr of the diesel engine,
at the grinding downshift of gears and the chirp

of airbrakes braking. Before the door folds
unfold and passengers begin to disembark,
you realize you do not want to let your mother

go alone into this high northern night
through mountain passes, frozen wheat fields,
past oil rigs pumping their thin elbows

in the dark. But she grabs the nearest
passenger, the scruffy-bearded, nose-pierced
boy with hair dyed jet-black, just like yours

was in the eighties and begins to drill him—
Is it warm on the bus? Are there seats available?
Is the driver nice?—which, he answers

to your amazement, tossing his smoke
to the sidewalk in a splash of sparks,
making you realize your mother

would be an excellent person to have along
at a rock concert or the holocaust or any
huge natural disaster, this survivor,

who grabs her floral bag to board the steps
not looking back, as you watch her
through smoky glass, moving down the aisle,

checking each seat row-by-row, with those eyes
that always saw everything, until she chooses
the best one, left side, one row behind the driver,

and stashes her bag, never once glancing down
at you, below in the cold, waving *goodbye,*
be careful, waving *safe travels,* waving *love you.*

Even as the driver downshifts, your mother
leans forward to chat—dark silhouette of her hand
on the headrest—even as he undoes the brake,

turns off the interior light and the bus jerks
to a start, you realize you are still waving, waving,
waving at the darkness now, waving at the spot

where you imagine she must be sitting.

COUPLES TRAVELING

Worse than traveling alone is to be stranded in security
behind couples, especially old traveling couples, now jacket

and vestless as they fuss shoeless in stocking feet, turn belts,
wallets in their hands as if newly-invented things. Torture

to wait by the conveyor, watch the wife pair and unpair
their shoes, zip and unzip her carry-on, which *she* wanted

to check, but, *no,* he refused. Almost to enter the dust
of their bedroom, to stand invisible on the plush carpet

by the bedside where they read by lamplight, discuss bosses,
bills and children, all grown now, like the daughter who delivered

the grandkids they are going to visit or the son who drove them
to the airport at early light. Even as the husband enters

the metal detector, you know his pockets are full of loose coins
and chewing-gum aluminum, just as the wife's suitcase contains

liquids too large and numerous for the baggies. What to do
but return them again and again through the X-ray, followed by

pat downs and manual searches. You'll hear about this later
when you find them occupying the seats next to you on the plane

where the husband will grab the male end of his seat belt
and attempt to slot it into your female strap, where a cell phone

will ring, loud and buried in the folds of their carry-on,
even as the plane taxis the runway, even as the wife digs deep

and answers, *yes, dear, we're on the plane*, even as the husband smiles
and takes full command of your rightful half of the armrest.

TRAVELING WITH GUITAR

For you can travel with a screaming red rolling bag
and float unnoticed on conveyors, through terminals

or you can lug half a moose rack from Maine
to Minnesota, carry it like a broken wing through airports

as my friend Gro did, and draw only the curious touches
of children waiting at gates. But dare to travel with a guitar

and invite confessions from strangers in pinstripe suits
of garage band summers, invite winks, *gotcha* smiles,

and devil's horns *rock-on* gestures. Invite finger points
and winks, the long tongue licks, and the rubberneck glance

to check if you are someone famous. To dare to travel
with a guitar is to mark yourself charismatic megafauna

of the airport terminal. Old friend, what else could I do
but carry you? I have stored you in closets, propped you

in corners, hunched over you late-nights, staring perplexed
at the mysteries of your neck. Body of my body, string

of my strings, see how the world began to hum and sing
that day at thirteen when I opened the big birthday box.

DOOR-TO-DOOR

Within minutes we were in the bedroom.
        I know this sounds bad.
Worse still to admit I'd said, *Sure,*
        come on over, when the man
called to inform me I was the lucky winner
        of a ten-piece set of cutlery.

So the stranger with sharp knives arrived
        in a green plaid polyester blazer
carrying a silver Kirby vacuum cleaner
        and a suitcase full of accessories
including this clear Petrie dish attachment
        lined with a cotton wafer, thin as a host,

that connected to the vacuum's hose
        to demonstrate, in one quick stroke
all the dust mites and dried skin cells
        the salesman could extract
from my curtains, couch, and mattress.
        Which is how we ended up

on our hands and knees in the bedroom
        with him asking, *Do you really want to live*
in this filth? And me answering, *Well, yes,*
        because I didn't have eight hundred dollars
or whatever ridiculous amount of money
        a Kirby cost in 1983. I'll admit

I feigned interest to justify accepting
            the cutlery, then I hedged to get him
out the door, which he read as my willingness
            to negotiate, saying, *Ho, ho, lady,*
you sure drive a hard bargain, leading to
            a succession of calls to his manager

waiting in some supervisor underworld,
            whom he harangued over my tan,
wall-mounted princess telephone, negotiating
            this once-in-a-lifetime, heretofore-unseen
bargain-basement price with such ruthless persuasion
            it required the manager to hang up

and consult his own fictitious supervisor.
            As the phone shrilled off my kitchen wall—
offer following counter offer—my brutish boyfriend
            was raised from the basement
where he was practicing guitar
            or masturbating or sneaking in calls

to his next girlfriend. And at first sight
            of my boyfriend's Black Irish eyes
the salesman gulped and exited with the Kirby
            and his suitcase of accessories,
recognizing in those eyes a brand of mean
            it would take me years to identify.

So maybe I did fill out a simple form
            offering my name, address,
and phone number for the lucky chance
            to win a membership at a local gym
or a cherry red Corvette or whatever
            worthless thing I desired

enough to slip all my information
            into a Plexiglas box at the mall.
These days I don't answer a door or a call
            unless I know exactly who lurks
on the other side of the wall.
            I think about that Kirby sometimes

wonder how it might have improved
            my situation. Mostly, I hope nobody
is forced to sell shit door-to-door
            in these inhospitable times. Even when
the salesman returned three days later
            to retrieve the green plaid polyester blazer

he'd left behind, on purpose or in haste—
            I admit I was short with him.
Even after he fished the Polaroid
            from his pocket to show me his kids,
a toddler and an infant in highchairs,
            chubby faces smeared red

with spaghetti-o's, even then
        I was not moved to buy the machine.
The princess phone is in a landfill somewhere,
        returned to the elements by now,
and the boyfriend, well,
        he got what he deserved.

A Kirby is a good investment, I still maintain,
        if you have that kind of disposable income.
But the knives in the end proved worthless.
        The handles, cheaply made,
and the blades never sharp enough
        when it finally came time to use them.

BALANCE

1.

Too careful, that first day, we sat on the floor palm-to-palm making church steeples. He showed me the trick where two can lean back-to-back in mid-air and rest easy, if one does not press harder than the other.

2.

Leaving his building that afternoon, I saw a full moon rising in the east, a cool blue wafer, like an offering in the sky; and the sun, an exhausted swimmer, disappeared into the orange pool of the west. I thought, if only I could reach up and cup both of them in my palms, I would feel certain.

3.

Today he comes in happy with some things from his apartment, things we can use—a cheese grater, a spatula, a red soup ladle. He pulls the utensils from the box and turns them in the air, one-by-one like a magician—a potato peeler, a pancake turner—before placing them in the drawer by the stove. I sit on the floor keeping track, I realize, for the day when I will again have to separate them from my own.

ECDYSIS

The female lobster waits by the den
of the largest male, wafts perfume
in his direction, the invitation to mate

or be eaten. Boxing proceeds until
she rests her pincers on his head,
a sign of readiness. Only she

knows when to secrete the enzyme
that exuviates her shell, splits it open
like a too-small suit, to slough off

the old carapace, a process named
after the Greek, *ekdysis,* meaning
"getting out." What happens next

in the watery room, no one likes to
talk about—except to marvel how
it's worked for 500 million years—

but I've read that she surrenders
her soft parts to him, then rests
under his protection for weeks

turning in milky strands of softness
until her hard shell returns, the chitin
of armor growing back like a tunic.

That they rise to part without
a backward glance is only human
whimsy to report. From birth,

lobsters know how to escape
the outgrown by tattooing
a replica of the exoskeleton

onto soft tissue. Tracing each follicle
and mandible, every section of spine
and pigment like a blueprint,

they withdraw blood from claws,
calcium from the spent shell.
Storing resources in gastroliths

along stomach walls, they wait
in murky depths for the imperceptible
sign to drink saltwater, enough to swell

the body, force off the old cage.
How difficult, this reverse birth,
threading the meat of claws backwards

through collapsed narrow joints,
then floating away from the shipwreck
with new antennae, gills, mouth, eyes.

LAZER LAND OUTING WITH BOYS

I'm not the boys' mother, although the picture
of us so convinces the arcade manager
that he shouts, *Happy Mother's Day,*

the moment we storm the entrance,
escaping the rain—these two blond boys,
their dark-haired father, and me,

the female free radical attached to
this all-male atom. Quirks of custody
result in the boys spending Mother's Day

with their father, and Father's Day
with their mother, who is presently
in Chicago having lunch or skiing

in the Sierra Nevada or possibly
snorkeling off the coast of Bermuda.
Pot roasts are simmering somewhere

but not in our kitchens. *Decided to*
take Mom out on her special day?
The arcade manager persists.

I should correct him. Truth is,
the weather's been bad, television
worse, church is out of the question,

and short of killing each other
we've elected this morning to hurl
basketballs through electronic hoops,

and grip careening wheels of arcade race cars,
our feet heavy on the accelerators
as we pass through movie landscapes

where we can lose the road, spin out,
roll over and walk away unscathed.
Now, it's time for the heavy artillery—

flak jackets with velcro straps, combat
helmets, power packs, and lazer pistols
with hair-sensitive triggers in our palms.

Do we want teams, the attendant
asks us, *or every man for himself?*
We look at the boys. Teams, they nod,

the big people against the little.
The attendant powers up the computer,
a small whine rising from its belly

spreads through our power packs
and pistols, our chests and torsos
light up our fluorescent patches

that mark the targets worth hitting,
the tender spots only those we love can see.
Be good to Mom now, the attendant says,

still misunderstanding. We enter
the dark cave of the shooting gallery,
where we will lie in wait behind barriers,

roll, tumble, and dodge. Where we will
lurk on one knee and search the dark,
then take aim, as only family can.

WHAT I LEARNED FROM PLAYING HEARTS

Nothing counts until the first heart is broken,
although the queen of spades can do damage anytime.
No one's likely to get hurt on the first move,
so if you have a profusion of spades, keep her near.

Although the queen of spades can do damage anytime,
better to hold trouble close, rather than wonder,
so if you have a profusion of spades, keep her near.
Remember, diamonds and clubs count for nothing—

better to hold trouble close, rather than wonder.
Begin by exhausting your weakest suit,
remember, diamonds and clubs count for nothing,
and try pawning off your hearts on others.

Begin by exhausting your weakest suit,
watch for people who keep changing the subject,
and try pawning off your hearts on others.
Beware of players who attempt to do the same to you.

Watch for people who keep changing the subject,
although evasion only works for so long.
Beware of players who attempt to do the same to you:
eventually someone's got to pay for the queen.

Although evasion only works for so long,
sometimes it's good to have an abundance of trouble:
eventually someone's got to pay for the queen;
and if you're in too deep, you can try to shoot the moon.

Sometimes it's good to have an abundance of trouble:
no one's likely to get hurt on the first move,
and if you're in too deep, you can try to shoot the moon.
Nothing counts until the first heart is broken.

GROUND OREGANO

Bitter green, bottled dust of pungent woods
I've carried across cities and states, past its prime,

almost gone now, *origanum vulgare.* Twenty-five years
since I tucked it deep in the spice rack after he insisted

he was allergic, although I'd used it in the lasagna,
chili, and spaghetti he'd eaten without illness

or complaint, so I guessed he was lying to make
a fuss, just as he invented a problem with dust

that required me to do the cleaning, and a fear
of mechanics and shopkeepers that made groceries

and oil changes my job. Just as he interrupted
every story I told with words like *ostensibly*

and *presumably,* because he was a spoiled first son
of a fussy mother who interviewed every teacher,

every piano and guitar tutor she hired as if he were heir
to the throne of Antigua. Eventually, I pinched

the bitter green into everything, then fled with the vial,
filed all these years behind my cinnamon, thyme,

and cumin. Even now, I see it on the back shelf,
unusable, almost spent, *Oros ganos,* from the Greek,

meaning, *joy on the mountain*. When fresh and strong
oregano can numb the tongue, make difficult words

unsayable. What have I neglected to mention?
His mother was his first grade teacher. Each day

they'd walk to school carrying matching briefcases.
After school, they sat together at the kitchen table.

While she prepared lesson plans, he busied himself
marking in red the erroneous papers of his classmates.

SCENT

That Christmas Eve
we watched Mother open present
after present, useful socks, a colorful blouse, cotton pajamas,

waited for the jeweled bottle
to rise from its wrapping, for the *ooh*s
and *aah*s and *you shouldn't have*s. Fragrance of juniper, sage,

narcissus. Through frosted
drugstore windows, two weeks earlier,
we'd spied Father turning amber bottles in the air, watched him

hand money to the lady
behind the counter. We'd felt smug
knowing what Mother was getting, she who kept our gifts

hidden in the cedar chest
under the airtight box with her tulle veil,
crushed rose bouquet, and ivory dress with its row of satin buttons.

What happened
to the extravagant gift, my sister and I
must have wondered, then neglected to ask, then forgot we ever knew.

Perfume disperses in layers,
over time. Hint of mandarin, lavender,
sandalwood. The top note is volatile and brilliant, a whiff of citrus,

quick to meet the nose
then evaporate. The heart note
is often flowery, the familiar body of the scent, a whisper of hyacinth

or violet. The base note
contains the heaviest molecules,
ongoing and slow to develop, containing the questions of musk and earth.

THUGS

Rather than write the memo
about the troubling colleague,
I go out to weed the flowerbed,
beat back the carpet of grass
that's overgrown its boundary,
search under the green and red
explosion of roses, behind blue spires
of delphinium for the surreptitious
sprigs of the pink evening primrose
that I formally removed from this bed
seasons ago, after I discovered
it gossiped about the blazing star,
overran the coreopsis, choked back
the dianthus. The mother plant
has been compost years now,
still her opportunistic runners
thread beneath the surface, spread
tendrils, blossoms, seeds. Beware
the blushing flower you invite into
your midst. Just like the sweet mint
I once thought it lovely to include
in the pot of basil, thyme, oregano,
rosemary, until it choked back
anything else green. Some things
must control every academic inch.
Thugs, they're called, garden thugs.

Too late before I realized
how she worked against me,
threw underground shoots,
spread stalks in the dark,
even in deadly silent winter
even while all around me
pretended to sleep.

SOME THINGS ABOUT THAT DAY

The placards I walked through. Wet raincoat on a hook. Questionnaire on a clipboard placed before me. Couples sat around me in the waiting room. They were young. What am I saying? I was only thirty-two.

But I remember, the men seemed the more bereft. Facing forward, their elbows resting on knees, their faces covered with hands. Or pushed back hard in the seats, gazing at a spot on the floor, legs stretched out in the aisles.

Difficult to remember the order in which things happened. The clipboard taken away, my name was called—our names were all called, the waiting room emptying and filling. Small orange pill in a tiny plastic cup. Water for washing it down. I was led to another room.

The gown that tied at the back, the bright fluorescent light, the posters with diagrams on the walls. Plenty of time to look around. The sound of vacuuming in another room.

The doctor arrives, hurried and unfriendly. Her one day in this clinic, she's flown in from another state. Death threats follow her. She asks me if I want to proceed. I tell her, *yes*. I lie back in the stirrups. The apparatus arrives—a silver canister on wheels with gauges and hoses attached to a long, cylindrical tube, thin like a spout. The sound of vacuuming close now. The nurse by my side, holding my shoulder. The doctor working away behind the thin film of my gown.

A blank space surrounds this moment. Sleepy from the sedative, yes, and numb. But let me not gloss over it. A feeling of tugging, mild discomfort. When the vacuum stops, the doctor asks if I want to know the sex. I tell her, *no*.

When I informed my husband I was pregnant, he said, *Is it mine?*
Not the best beginning. We'd been married a month. Married on
Leap Day. Who else's could it be? He had an important meeting at work
that day, some critical task. I had driven myself.

Sleep, after the procedure. (My friend tried to soften it for me afterwards.
Just say you had a procedure, dear.) Nothing about it was procedural. I woke
in a room of sleeping beauties. Afterwards, cramping, nausea. Faint, when
I woke up, dizzy.

Orange juice and back down for twenty minutes. And then the odd
assemblage of street clothes smoothed onto my limbs, the parting advice
from the nurse, the script for a prescription pushed into my hand. Strange to
walk out the door. The protesters gone. My car started just fine, slipped right
into gear. I backed out, went forward. Drove light-headed to the drugstore.

At the pharmacy, the man in the white coat looked at me when I handed
him the script. Could he see from the prescription where I'd been? A
softness dawned on his face. *Go home,* he said. They would deliver it.

Only then, in the car, did I start to cry. So stupid. Over the kindness of the
pharmacist. When I got home, my husband was on the couch, watching
the NBA playoffs. Even before the drugs arrived—even after—he couldn't
stop telling me what a brave girl I had been.

WARRIOR

So this student whose haircut makes him look like a sharp
fraternity man, this student with a hatchet nose and eyes

like a watchful eagle, really, even in poetry class, who wears
a volleyball uniform to school because practice immediately

follows prosody, who writes poems about patrols and dust offs
and how his wife won't listen as they lie in bed after making love,

and I, too, have not been listening closely enough to this student
who writes poems about the shrapnel embedded in his right thigh

and scars and things he had to do in the dirt and heat. And still
I am blind and thinking these are such good historical poems,

persona poems, really good World War II poems, until I see
words like *collateral damage*, until I see IEDs and desert imagery,

not jungle imagery, then I realize, no, I have been mistaken,
this is not Vietnam, not the South Pacific, this is the next generation

of warriors we have sent to do our work, groomed to come back
wounded, guilty, dead, silent, or full of stories that no one is willing

to sit still long enough to listen to, or hear told, this well or truly.

NIL DUCTILITY

Time now to wonder about Bruce who sold
laminated timber beams out of his Fargo office,
the old growth forested in Oregon and East Glacier,

then planed, bent, glued, and shipped cross-country
from Montana in semis. The Douglas fir arches
and load-bearing trusses that supported the canopies

and curved interiors of tall churches, office buildings,
and shopping malls—all the gracious spaces where hallowed
work is done. Winter afternoons in the eighties I'd sluice

from campus through the snow in my Fury to his office,
Building Supplies, Inc., and sit in the second desk,
across the room, as Bruce took complaints, argued

with architects, calculated lineal feet. I'd type, file,
read my schoolbooks when my desk was empty,
then talk across the room after all the estimates

were faxed. It was Bruce who taught me about nil ductility
after my Fury broke down at twenty-below zero,
explaining how even steel has its limits, in extremes,

becomes brittle and shatters, rather than bending
or deforming as it would in normal temperatures.
Even then, Bruce was going blind from MS,

from exposure to chemicals during his tours
with the 79th Combat Engineers. Even then,
sometimes he'd call me over to read the fine print,

and sometimes at the end of the day, he'd pull open
his bottom drawer, remove the pack of photographs,
some faded color, some black-and-white, all frayed

and graying at the edges, ringed with a rubber band
which he'd remove with careful fingers, then hand
to me, one image at a time, describing the concussion

of the blown bunker, the green sandbags raining
down, how the white femur and tibia of his friend
shattered like fractured timber from a land mine.

The photos were contraband, he explained,
yet all the GIs took them, smuggled the film
out of country to be developed, then stored

for safekeeping after the war. By the eighties
the photos were stashed in lockboxes and offices
where wives and children would not find them.

How many times did he hand me the framed
glossy smile of his younger self on leave
in Da Nang, beer in hand, arm thrown over

a buddy, ready to ship for R & R in Singapore.
How many times did I hold in my hands
the flat profile of the Vietcong—the open eyes

and the swollen lips of the boy who attacked
their camp that night, whose skin was bruised gray
and buzzing with flies by morning, whose body

lay on the periphery in mud until first light made it safe
for the GIs to come out and discover the identity
of their attacker. Rare to see the enemy, he said,

so they were amazed to roll him over and find
this boy—his body so thin, his small hands,
his young face, all they could do was circle him

and take these photographs, like the one we held
in our hands. I looked, because I thought I should.
I listened because he needed me to, still bearing

all that weight so many years later, the pressure
reducing him, I could see, even as we sat together
in the dwindling light at Building Supplies, Inc.

GROUND ZERO

SMALL BURIED THINGS

1. Silos

ground zero   we believed
        we were   ground zero
                north dakota, 1964

minute men sleeping in silos   by the thousands
we knew   we couldn't say   we didn't know

ICBMs pockmarking the landscape
encased in concrete silos   six stories deep
buried in pastures
surrounded by cyclone wire
where holsteins muzzled through
for ungrazed grass

silos   bordering wheatfields
where farmers passed close by
with plows   seeders   combines
watched by soldiers
year round   in uniform   rifles in hand

small buried things   the great mirror underworld
grain silos above   missile silos below

        some people said they felt safer
        some said it helped the local economy
        some liked the men the missiles brought to town

there were launch command centers
disguised as family ranch houses
sprinkled around the countryside

       the basketball hoop above the garage door
       the radio tower on the roof
       the army jeep parked in the drive
       the chain-link fence around the perimeter

and below ground   deep concrete bunkers
where launch sequences were memorized
by the buried few   the survivors
       those who would avenge us
        at the ready   to strike   after we were obliterated

for decades   they memorized codes   protocols   launch sequences
       controlling the cluster of ten missiles each at their command

we knew   we couldn't say   we didn't know

but look around you   to the west   minot air force base
       to the east   grand forks air force base
        how many air bases does one state need?

only the best get stationed up north, the airmen said
       what else could they say about drawing the short straw
        the assignment in siberia   surely
          they'd offended someone as powerful as stalin
          to be shipped here

strategically located   we were told
we were strategic   russia

not as far away as it might seem
one quick arc over the ice cap
north dakota to moscow

the shortest line between two points   they told us
          the small converging world
                    of the arctic circle

we knew   we couldn't say   we didn't know

ground zero   years later   we learned
          north dakota would have been the third largest
                    nuclear power in the world

 if we'd seceded from the union

2. Chill Factor

sometimes at parties in moorhead
my friend's late night rambling
hushed   as if fearing microphones
in the walls   crazy talk, really
about what was buried
in the countryside   up north

everyone gone from the party   just a few of us
slumped deep in couches
blowing smoke rings
the night's music playing   on repeat

the cup from the keg's last beer
warm in our hands   my friend would begin
the story   again   it never varied
about his late night drive
          up north   years ago   three a.m.
                    twenty below   outside, the chilblain night
                              the darkened eyelids of farmhouses

inside the car   the radio playing soft rock, he said
the DJ's distant voice   the heater blasted
yet the windshield stayed cold to the touch

above   the full moon
          large and bright in the sky
                    so illuminated the icy fields
                              he could have driven without headlights

lunacy, really   what he says happened next
on the horizon   he saw

a sparkle of light   break   in the distance
        from a timid crack in the earth   an aperture
            something heavy opened   a beacon
                spread   in the night   then a nose emerged

soundless   first, a tip   then a slim column lifted up   revealed itself

foot by foot   a minuteman
pulling clean from its shell
a needle unthreading itself

sparks followed   soundless   lifting in a spitting arc above
then growing small   out of sight   lost among the stars

he said   he barely kept the car on the road
he said   his hands spun the radio dial
            through talk & jazz
            all the late-night-preaching about   salvation
            fire & brimstone   end-of-days   revelation

he says   he scanned pop   rock   country
white noise   up and down the dial
he searched   for the breaking news
waiting to hear about the impact   what part of the world had fallen silent
but only the chatter continued   all night
he criss-crossed the roads and circled the dial

he knew   he didn't know   he said   he couldn't say

what he had seen   that cold winter night
in the high, north   middle of nowhere
he drove the backroads until dawn, he said
waiting for the world to end.

3. Frack

first the bakken   then the three forks formation   even deeper
    the oil patch, they call it
        two miles below the surface

oil embedded in shale
late devonian   remnants of the anoxic sea   the coastal carbonite layer
deposited when the middlewest was inner ocean

four hundred billion barrels, estimated   rest there   perhaps more   light and tight
the largest oil find in north american history
    conflict-free oil, they say
    ending the dominance of energy-rich rogue nations

the boom began in montana, alberta
    then spread to north dakota
        drawn within our borders
            by a friendly change to the state tax code

now eleven thousand wells pump
    a million barrels a day
        thirty thousand new workers converging on small towns
        people housed in man camps
        mostly good people, some desperate, some dangerous

the talk is about the rise in crime—robberies, stabbings, domestic disputes
    a sydney woman, early morning jogger, mother and math teacher
    grabbed from the side of the road
    later found strangled

the murderers bought a shovel at walmart to bury her
    then returned it for a refund later
        that's how the police caught them

so, the talk centers on the observable
    the damage to infrastructure
    the eyesore roads where there were no roads before
    the old highways, pitted and full of potholes undriveable dangerous
    the speed of the oil and water trucks on the public roads
    the rise in highway fatalities

to frack you must drill down
    through topsoil, stratum, sedimentary rock
        down through fresh water aquifers,
            to reach the dolomite the source rock

drill vertically then horizontally to reach the shale
    injecting millions of gallons of water per frack
        laced with hundreds of chemicals (some of them linked to cancer)
            most of them proprietary to corporations
            unknowable to ordinary citizens

unaskable, since the halliburton loophole (of 2005)
    exempted fracking from protections guaranteed to all citizens
        in the safe drinking water act (of 1974)

we knew we couldn't say we didn't know

except what's certain—benzene, toluene, ethylbenzene, and xylene
    volatile organic compounds
        and diesel fuel (around 1 percent per gallon) used on the bakken shale

plus, the radium inert in the rocks
brought back up in the fracking fluid
after it's made its long journey below to gather the oil
then brought topside to be separated out

and shipped to a wastewater center where it's *treated   cleaned*
    in condensate tanks, some of them lined, some unlined
        seeping into the ground, toxins evaporating into the air

what's left over, uncleanable
    trucked in water tankers to be disposed of   *reinjected*
        in the land previously known as away.

4. Quake

beyond groundwater contamination
    now earthquakes in colorado, arkansas
        the swath of states between alabama and montana

a sixfold increase over twentieth-century levels
    at least a dozen quakes last year in northern ohio
        one measuring up to 4.8 on the richter scale

speculation about the 30,000 disposal sites around the country
    where fracking wastewater is deposited
        reinjected for final disposal
            into a deeper layer known as basement rock

speculation about fracking itself
    the deep underground explosions to extract oil
        the water causing shifting plates, lubricating faults

look for damage to homes
look for reports of contaminated drinking water
look for increases in breast cancer, miscarriages, birth defects

we knew   we couldn't say   we didn't know   ground zero

and this just in: the air force reports
        150 minutemen silos still rest underground
        honeycombed deep below
        in northwestern north dakota
        embedded in the fracking zone

the commander of the air base says,
    we certainly can co-exist with the oil industry

the petroleum council vice president says,
  we're communicating about how we share our territory
the air force commander reports,
  the drilling frenzy has presented no ill-effects to the ICBMs

ultra-sensitive instruments possessed by the air force, we are assured
    can detect seismic activity as far away as mexico
        capable of tracking even the slight vibrations
            caused by the simplest of thunderstorms

5. Lament

north dakota   i'm worried about you
the companies you keep   all these new friends   north dakota
    beyond the boom, beyond the extraction of precious resources
        do you think they care what becomes of you

north dakota   you used to be the shy one
enchanted secret land loved by only a few   north dakota

when i traveled away and told people i belonged to you   north dakota
    your name rolled awkwardly from their tongues
        a mouth full of rocks, the name of a foreign country

north dakota   you were the blushing wallflower
the natural beauty, nearly invisible, always on the periphery
north dakota   *the least visited state in the union*

now everyone knows your name   north dakota
the blogs and all the papers are talking about you   even *60 minutes*
i'm collecting your clippings   north dakota
the pictures of you from space
    the flare ups in your northern corner
        like an exploding supernova
            a massive city where no city exists
                a giant red blight upon the land

and those puncture wounds   north dakota   take care of yourself
the injection sites   i see them on the maps
eleven thousand active wells   one every two miles

all your indicators are up   north dakota
    four hundred billion barrels, some estimates say
        more oil than we have water to extract
            more oil than we have air to burn

north dakota   you could run the table right now   you could write your own ticket
    so, how can i tell you this?   north dakota, your politicians

        are co-opted (or cowards or bought-out or honest and thwarted)
            they're lowering the tax rate for oil companies
            they're greasing the wheels that need no greasing
            they're practically giving the water away
            they've opened you up and said, *take everything*

north dakota   dear sleeping beauty   please, wake up

        what will become of your sacred places,
        what will become of the prairie dog,
        the wolf, the wild horses, the eagle,
        the meadowlark, the fox, the elk,
        the pronghorn antelope, the rare mountain lion,
        the roads, the air, the topsoil,
        your people, your people,
        what will become of the water?

north dakota   who will ever be able to live with you
once this is all over   i'm speaking to you now
as one wildcat girl   to another   be careful   north dakota

WILD THYME

BUOY

And so you came to realize that a married man
is like a drowning victim, when you find him

drenched, adrift and unhappy in the vast ocean
of his marriage. And won't you always be the one

to spot him—a floating speck on the horizon,
flapping his arms for rescue, desperate mouth

ringing an O above the rolling crests and waves.
You on the high dry deck of the cruise ship

in your crisp white shorts and espadrilles.
Aren't you the beacon, aren't you the life preserver.

And when you jump into the sea salt foam,
if only for a refreshing swim, don't you understand

that he will seize upon you, strong buoyant
swimmer that you are, grab your shoulders,

pull your head under with his weight, so dense
in the water. And down among the reefs

and coral, with your new copper-coin eyes,
you will see then how he rides upon the shoulders

of his water-breathing sea horse wife,
and his mermaid mistresses, those water nymph

former lovers, and a whole tag-team pyramid
of three-breasted women who tried

over the years to save him. Even then,
next time, when you see another one

go under, does it give you pause,
does it stop you from jumping in—

no, not once, not ever.

WILD THYME

I took the photographs, naturally, as the other poets
fell backwards into wild thyme, too worried
about appearing the tourist or ruining my clothes

in the phryngana, the zone between mountain
and sea, wood and water. On the rented boat
to Antiparos, as the others slipped into wet suits,

pulled on squeaky flippers, rolled into azure depths
with Panayotis, the marine biologist, I stayed
on the moored boat with whiskery Captain Giorgos

nursing my salty old grudge against water.
On the south shore of the island, when invited
to sing into the mouth of the sea caves that echo

the ancient world back, I had only a pop tune
to offer (I can't bear to name it). Between Lefkes
and Marpissa, where the Byzantine trail empties

down to the sea, when the old man with hair
like a wild bird's nest and a toothless collapsing
chin saw me, an American, enter the chapel

he guarded, he shouted, *Ah, George Bush!*
and my only response was, *I didn't do it!*
(meaning, vote for him), which made all

the other Americans laugh. At Marathi,
where the mountain opens to marble quarries
so translucent that the Venus de Milo,

the temples on Delos, and Napoleon's tomb
are carved from it, as the guide distributed
the headlamps for our underground excursion,

he had to ask, *Now, is anyone here claustrophobic?*
And I had to answer, *Well, yes,* because
I would never depend upon tourists

to pull my limp and breathless body
from any dark crevasse. So I guarded
the entrance as the others descended,

sat back to study the guidebooks.
Did you know that 150,000 slaves mined
these quarries. They say a bas relief

above one opening depicts Pan cavorting
with Nymphs. Did you know the thyme
that grows on this mountainside feeds

bees that make rare, wild honey, the color
of amber. Aromatic and savory, they say,
with the taste of white pepper, dates, and fruit.

THE OUD

It traveled to me from Damascus
        shipped in a plywood box
resembling a baby's coffin.
        Inside the rough latches,
the tiny instrument's long thin neck,
        its bent-back pegbox,
and staved gourd of a stomach
        looked like the resting body
of a goose, exhausted
        from the forced migration
across the Atlantic and Mediterranean.

Forebear of the lute and guitar
        what hands must have played you
before my graceless fumblings,
        what ancient music sounded
through your strings. And how strange
        the moist new air must have seemed.

In truth, it did not last six months.
        First, the neck failed to hold
the instrument in tune. One-by-one
        the ribs sprang loose
from the pear-shaped soundbox.
        Soon, the spruce top
pulled free from the cavernous body
        as if something inside
the oud insisted on its freedom.

But that first morning
      something so odd
I now recall—
      when I burned sage,
passed a smudge over
      the instrument
to clear its path to this new life,
      as I turned to leave the room,
a note sounded from its strings,
      an audible note rang out
I swear. One note, loud and clear
      with no hand touching the neck
or strings, with not a pick
      or a plectrum in sight.

WHISKER MEDITATIONS

1.

When I told my fiancé's mother about my persistent, recurring whisker—lower right, underside of my chin—she smiled sideways, said, "Be glad it's only one."

2.

I was parked in the lot outside Bed, Bath & Beyond with my then-husband. I was applying lipstick in the mirror the first time I spotted it—my whisker enjoying a stretch of unchecked growth.

It was hot in the car. We were laughing. My husband tried to pull it out with his fingertips. When that failed, he offered to tweeze it with his teeth. What an act of extreme devotion. It makes me wonder why I ever let him go.

3.

It begins, a smooth bump on the skin that you must worry for days with your fingertips. Then, a small nub, slight friction in the follicle, nothing visible. Hours pass, days. You forget. Then one day you catch it in silhouette or sunlight—a long tendril like a pliable scrap of piano wire sprung from your chin.

4.

My friend Jenny tells me about one night after she and Colin made love. Lying there, sweaty, happy, Colin spotted a long brown hair on Jenny's chest—his hair, he thought. When he tried to pick it off, the skin lifted, the follicle resisted. It was connected. "Get it off me," Jenny screamed. "Get it off!"

5.

This sliver of iron ore spun from the lava core of the earth, one
thin chin wire rising through Cambrian, Devonian, up through
continental shelves, bedrock, shale, topsoil. This tendril—manganese,
copper, platinum—must have pierced my heel, threaded my first
step, wound around tendons, up shin, thigh, groin, traveled through
heart, breast, throat to arrive here on my chin in my fortieth year.

6.

Sometimes in meetings at work, I catch myself stroking my sad
whisker when contemplating problems. I better understand now
the gestures of my bearded colleagues who, over the years, have
cradled their chins, stroked with the grain, against the grain, or,
when really perplexed, vigorously scratched a stubbled cheek.

7.

In the bathroom of a four-star hotel—marble shower, terrazzo floors
—I turn on the lighted magnifying mirror hanging near the vanity.
Never mind crow's feet, enlarged pores, the natural exigencies of age.
        But, oh, in the magnifying glass, under that terrifying light
—constellations of age spots, catastrophe of eyebrows, oh, whisker! All
the while my fiancé is knocking on the frosted glass door. *What are you
doing in there?*

8.

And now my whisker has attracted an evil albino twin, emerging from the
doorway of the neighboring pore. How long, how long, will it be before the
rest of the family arrives—the older brother, the in-laws, and parents, not
to mention the car full of California cousins.

9.

To pluck it, you must stand by the window, blinds open in full light
with a tweezer and a hand mirror. Try to tuck yourself behind the
billow of the curtain. No need for you to star in a YouTube video
titled, "My Crazy Old Neighbor Lady Plucks Her Whisker Again."

10.

You'll never get it on the first try or the second. You have to poke
around. Then one day, the tweezer's edge will land, small suction as
the follicle releases. When it happens to me, I hold the whisker up in
the light, say, *Got it! You bastard!*

A small moment of satisfaction followed by silence, vacuous
air, contemplating the many hours and days, the many weeks it will
take for this grave act to be undone.

LAKE EFFECT

snow for days   let it
         the weather woman
                is always wrong   we rise

these pearl white mornings
            made warm by your long back
                east of lake michigan

unexpected   always coming
          great crystal flakes
             float outside your windows

white pine branches lowered
         heavy with snow   we rise
              to the meteorologist's apologies

this upland peninsula
        so shaped like a paw
            or an oven mitt

people will raise their hands
        a kind of swearing to
           and point to the spot

where they're from   this place
        in the heart of the palm
           where I found you

a bit left of center
        lake effect   people around here say
          to things that happen

all the things   wonderful or strange
        they can never hope to
                predict or explain.

ANOTHER DAY ON EARTH

Good morning, I shout to the powerwalker
who passes me on the boardwalk
because it's sunny and lakes country.

Yes, he says. *It's a good day to be above ground!*
He speaks out of the side of his mouth
like a tough guy or a stroke victim

or a tough guy who's survived a stroke
which brings Father to mind. I look down
to avoid the cracks between the slats.

Beside me, Lake Superior waves its heavy
blue arms. I watch the disappearing back
of the powerwalker. His headband matches

his wristbands—white terrycloth and tight.
His limp is quick, but not fast enough
for the ferocious pumping of arms.

His too tiny running shorts and tank top
reveal too much bruised and mottled skin
like parchment bearing signs of illness.

After my father died, the nerve of everything
that moved and breathed offended me
as he slept deep in a cold blue suit.

At the cemetery, as the casket lowered,
we all stared down in silence, except for
the whine of hydraulics. And the second

the gears ceased their crawling,
mourners turned and started talking
of weather and crops. I'm told Father

used to joke at funerals, *Why does someone
always have to die for us to get together?*
He was good at that. Better than me.

Laughing into the teeth of death.

MOTHER, IN PICTURES

mother, at two   propped on the running board
        of the brand new model t truck   swaddled
                in a black wool coat and fur hat   mother

posing by the peonies wearing a white crochet tam
        mother, outside   holding a ukulele   a baton   a baby doll

mother posing with tricycle   later, with bicycle
        mother in a black french beret
                mother posing in her good cotton school dress
                        behind her, the long unbroken horizon

        years later great aunt martha would say,
        your mother sure thought she got something when she had you

mother, at five   holding leroy, her baby brother   the one good day
        the blustery sky   his crying red eyes
                born in may, he died in november

mother with a wagon, hauling her dolls
        feeding the lambs with a nipple bottle
                posing with two white dogs   with a black horse

then a third child, another boy   mother was eleven
        the midwife told grandpa to go for a doctor
                twenty-five miles to napoleon, no doctor available
                thirty miles to steele, no doctor available

mother said she hid in the barn, covered her ears to muffle grandma's screams
        the boy was named donald
                born with a broken arm and collarbone
                he lasted two days

your mother sure thought she got something when she had you.

mother, in a white dress holding her lutheran catechism
       mother, in winter, twenty years old in a tight white sweater
           hugging her knees on the front steps
                  a windmill in the background   mother
                     she hasn't met any of us yet.

POOR YOU

Back when we were still together, it seemed
my ex-boyfriend could never lose anything.
Car keys, dollar bills, everything that fell from

his charmed pockets floated back. *Lucky us.*
Checkbooks dropped in grocery store parking lots
delivered to our front door by Good Samaritans

before the ice cream melted. Perhaps this is why
he treated me with such benign neglect, forgetting
how the slippery dime of me could work through

the stitches of silk pockets. Once, at the therapist's
he handed the Kleenex box to me with this look
on his face, *poor you,* like I was some catastrophe

under glass. *Oh, poor us.* It reminded me of a cartoon
I'd seen in the paper of two men in a sinking canoe.
The guy in the front end is submerged, taking in water,

already drowning. The guy in the back of the canoe
is tipped high and dry. In the caption, he's thinking,
Boy, am I glad I wasn't on that end of the boat.

INTEREST

To hold love in one's hands like capital
like a fluid animal, best in motion,

then pass it along with a bit skimmed off,
that's the theory of love and interest.

Last night in the dream my first husband
said, *I dream of you.* Odd in a dream to hear

what another dreams, odder still to receive
the offer so many years after the desire.

This is how love most resembles money,
everyone willing to give you the thing

most wished for, once it's no longer needed.
Like those sprinklers we ran through

during the downpour in the Bitterroots—
no one could tell us how to turn them off.

All night, in bed we heard them *fust, fust*
against dripping willows. The next morning,

the besotted lawn, the driver waiting.
Your hand on your heart, for lack of words,

as we kissed before our final parting.

TO THE WOMAN WHO TORE
THE WORD "HUSBAND" FROM
THE *OXFORD ENGLISH DICTIONARY*

Surely it was a wife who removed
the pages beginning with *hurtle*
and ending with *hush,* while the word,

husband, lurked somewhere in between,
ripped, judging from the jagged edges
and stuffed in a coat pocket

to be smuggled to a kitchen table,
to a fierce fight under glaring light,
to be read aloud and pointed at

and served up as solid evidence.
The missing pages now replaced
in grainy photocopy by some librarian,

so that other confused or angry
women can continue to check for
true meanings of the word. *Husband,*

finding its roots in "house" and
"bound," as in, a man who owns
his house and land, or the master

of the household (now obsolete),
or a tiller of the ground (also obsolete),
or a male animal kept for breeding

(rare, *OED* insists). In the history
of the language, he's had many names
and occupations—tiller of soil, cultivator,

the steward who manages his affairs
with skill and thrift. He's out there,
the husband, each day redefining

the word that follows *hurtless, hurtsome.*

MEMORABILIA

—Roger Maris Museum, West Acres Shopping Mall, Fargo, North Dakota

Across from Nails Pro and Forever 21
behind a corner of glass, Roger Maris
swings without ceasing and rounds bases
on an endless tape loop of home runs—
57, 58, 59, 60—leading to number 61
in the year 1961, the homer that broke
Babe Ruth's 1927 record. His trophies,
autographed baseballs, and signed bats
rest under a portrait of his golden beauty
near the display of authentic jerseys,
his Sultan of Swat crowns, and replicas
of a Yankees locker and stadium seat.
Maris died of lymphatic cancer at age 51
in a Houston hospital. "I still see him
in my dreams," Mickey Mantle said.
The Baseball Hall of Fame holds the ball
he hit off Tracy Stallard in the '61 Series,
his No. 61 bat, and his No. 9 Yankees
jersey, but his body was brought home
to Fargo to be buried on the north side
at the Holy Cross Cemetery on 32nd Avenue.
His tombstone, a square of black granite
mounted to resemble a baseball diamond.

BOOKMOBILE

To be saved by books, to be allowed to file
in twos away from Sister Paula's math class,

to climb those three small steps off the curb,
and be met by the smell of glue, old paper,

leather bindings. To lay my hands on
thin volumes with titles other than *The Lives*

of the Saints. A miracle, and that woman,
a saint, who steered the big wheel and roared

the loaded van to our school each Friday.
I do not recall the plots or the people

in those books, though I read them all—
every word in every book in each tall stack

I hauled in small arms down the steps,
making the final blind hop to the curb,

then back to the rigors of six times eight
equals. After school, I'd crawl into bed

with those books, the weight of them
spread all around me. Mother washed

the bedding each Friday, and the combination
was unbearable—heaven—pages turned

by unknown hands and the fresh air
smell of clean sheets. The rows of black words

on heavy paper, concrete proof of things
calling me from beyond the parochial.

PURSE

They say pickpockets brush past victims first
to observe the unconscious protective gesture.

Where the hand goes after soft contact reveals
the precise location of the wallet or passport.

Some memories from childhood, I'm realizing,
are no longer felt or known, but live only in poems

I wrote, stored there when memory still held
like a purse whose drawstrings I opened and closed.

My mother's dreams of my late father are often pecuniary.
En route to somewhere in the car, she realizes she forgot

her purse. *Don't worry,* he will say, *I have money.*
Who knows where love hides in the enclosures of marriage.

The first time my fiance's son sneezed and reached out
his hand for a tissue, I understood why mothers carry

such big purses. Because memory is a sieve, separating
the coarse from fine. Because memory is a seine, capturing

and releasing. My grandfather's brook trout—do I remember it
from the rainbow display as he posed beside the bright curtains

or from the snapshot Grandmother took for the album.
And the reedy timbre of my father's voice, can I retrieve it

as an acoustic artifact, a real thing my ear can still hear, or only
as the playback recording of my own voice, the copy he made

in me. *Oh goodness,* my cousin will say, when I go home to visit,
you sure have your father's mannerisms. It's a likeness people will observe,

but you could never see yourself. Then today, a strange thing—
playing with the puppies, I felt my lips pull into a purse,

a gesture to contain happiness too sweet and pure for release
into laughter. And I realized it's the look I saw on my father's face

watching me grow up. Only I wear it now in my own body,
this time, inside-out, I can see it—the expression of my father's love.

NEWS FLASH

"This is a substantial find as diamonds of this size are a very rare occurrence,"
Nare's CEO Charles Mostert said.
— *Mail & Guardian*, April 22, 2006

One cape yellow diamond, octahedron-shaped, 235 carats,
was found in the Schmidstdrift mine, an alluvial riverbed

outwash near Kimberley, South Africa, by a three-week-old
start-up company named Nare Diamonds Limited, who re-opened

the mine—closed for three years by the previous company,
(unnamed, in all accounts) who labored there for years,

who went bankrupt mining gems of 1.14 carats or less.
The report says, twenty-one days after resuming work

in the Schmidstdrift, Nare Diamonds found the 235 carat
diamond, cape yellow, octahedron, the size of a hen's egg,

rough-cut and shining amidst the mine's erosion deposits.
This small morning news flash, scrolling across my screen,

returns me to my desk, to the bottom left drawer,
to the gray-green notebook, and what lies buried there.

BACK WHEN WE ALL GOT ALONG

Everyone's thinner, less worn in the face.
The children are all on the wrong laps.
Disorderly pyramid of family, spreading

up the front steps. The sun is bright,
the lawn so green. Father grasps
the wrought iron rail on the top landing,

usual amused smirk, usual waistband
pulled high under armpits. Mother looks
so young, a sister among daughters.

The smallest grandson squirms on her lap.
Wish I could insert myself beside them,
missing all those years, on the road

playing music. My brother-in-law, Al,
is missing too, probably visiting family
in Oakes. And my second-oldest sister

has said something funny from behind
the camera to get the kids to make faces—
stuck-out tongues, googly-eyed monsters.

Grandma stands on the lawn beside them—
a delighted smile, her hands folded over
her stomach. Gotthelf is with her,

the man she married after Grandpa died,
who is already senile or soon will be.
Soon, too, three children for my brother

and his young wife. Plus, the discovery
that the other brother-in-law, the one
posed high on the landing with Father,

is using more than his fine carpentry skills
to renovate the kitchen, bathroom, deck,
and sunroom of the woman in town

with the traveling husband. But not today,
today looks perfect, except for the wrinkle
of the youngest daughter's absence.

I want to bless them from this distance.
Debbie is like the wind, they often say of me,
You never know when she will blow into town.

CHINA: 5,000 YEARS

—Guggenheim Exhibition, 1998

not the jade ornament of a pig-dragon   or the lamp in the shape of a goose holding a fish
    not the bronze buckle ornament of a dancer with cymbals
        or the nephrite jade carving of a winged horse
            all from the 2nd century BC

not the chime with a crouching dragon carving from 1600 BC
    or the rearing gilt bronze dragon from the 8th century

not the Neolithic goblet with eggshell walls so delicate
    or the eleven-headed bust of Avalokitesvara, looking eleven times compassionate
        or the Buddhist ritual objects—a carved turtle, a pillbox

not the Ming dynasty silk paintings with mountains that look like dragons
    or the earthenware squatting musician with dimples and a drum from 25 BC
    who looks as modern as the busker you saw on the street today

not the dragon-shaped jade pendants from the 4th century BC
    that make you wonder about the marvelous lapels or blouses
        of the ancient people who could have worn such things

which gets you thinking about the cave of your own people
    where they must have been squatting at that time
        drinking out of streams, gnawing meat off bones
            with no clock or mirror or comb or pen
                or compass or gilded silver tea utensils
                    certainly, not even tea or calligraphy

none of this hits you until the Indian restaurant on Columbus Avenue
    where you sit by a big window and watch the stream of faces push by

and perhaps you've had too much wine, and garlic naan, and mughlai chicken
        and maybe the ragas aren't helping either, the sitars and tablas
            circling around a five-note melody

and that's when something starts to well up in you
        —you hope you can make it back to the hotel—
so you ask the waiter for your bill, but instead
        he brings you dessert, a small custard in an oval bowl
which he offers in cupped hands for your inspection
        saying, *for you, on the house*

and you try to say *thank you,* to register your delight
        but instead, something starts to come out, a deluge
tears now, the napkin clutched to your face
        mascara smeared on white linen
and real crying, real shoulder-rocking sobs

all of which alarms the waiter, who has bent down to you now
        and the two women dining in the table next to you
have rushed to your side asking, *is it something we said?*
        No, no, between sobs, you try to tell them
about the exhibit of 5,000 years of Chinese history
        about the smooth five-petaled porcelain bowl from the 10th century
and the funerary objects carved in the shapes of laughing dogs

but all you can get out, really, is the thing about the terra cotta warriors
        the soldier, the military officers, the general, and the horse and cart
that represent the other 6,000 figures discovered in Pit 1 in the Shaanxi province,
        the way they looked so lost in the Guggenheim without their spears, swords,
or crossbows, with their hands still frozen after centuries as if holding weapons

but mostly, it was their faces—
      how you realized real people must have posed for each statue,
real people from 200 BC, each with unique noses, hair plaits,
      shapes of eyes, curves of cheekbone—
and how they were all so dead now, how they'd all been dead
      for such an incredibly long time.

NOTES

"SMALL BURIED THINGS"

The long poem, "Small Buried Things," draws details from many recent articles and news reports. Events in the North Dakota oil patch have developed at a fast pace, so news articles can be found daily about the oil boom. Below is a listing of the articles and media sources that were consulted in the writing of the poem.

"Air Force: N.D. Oil Drilling Poses No Threat to Underground Nuclear Missiles." *Twincities.com* 12 Apr. 2012. <http://www.twincities.com/ci_20384362/air-force-n-d-oil-drilling-poses-no>

Battistoni, Alyssa. "Does Fracking Cause Earthquakes?" *Blue Marble: Mother Jones* 16 Apr. 2012. <http://www.motherjones.com/blue-marble/2012/04/does-fracking-cause-earthquakes>

Behar, Michael. "Whose Fault?" *Mother Jones* March/Apr. 2013: 32–64.

Crude Independence. Documentary. Dir. Noah Hutton. 2009. DVD.

Dobb, Edwin. "The New Oil Landscape." *National Geographic.* Mar. 2013: 26–59.

Donovan, Lauren. "Helms says EPA Could Halt Fracking in Oil Patch." *Bismarck Tribune* 27 Nov. 2011. <http://bismarcktribune.com/news/state-and-regional/helms-says-epa-could-halt-fracking-in-oil-patch/article_fe9a3284-18b9-11e1-ba39-001cc4c03286.html>

Gasland. Documentary. Dir. Josh Fox. 2010. DVD.

Gasland II. Documentary. Dir. Josh Fox. 2013. DVD.

Jervin, Sara. "The Fracking Frenzy's Impact on Women." The Center for Media and Democracy's PR Watch. 4 Apr. 2012. <www.prwatch.org/news/2012/04/11204/fracking-frenzys-impact-women>

Johnson, Robert. "Strippers Can Earn $350,000 A Year In This Oil Boomtown Club." *Business Insider* 17 Jan. 2013 <www.businessinsider.com/williston-north-dakota-oil- boomtown-high-paying-stripper-demand-2013-1?op=1>

Manning, Richard. "Bakken Business: The Price of North Dakota's Fracking Boom." *Harpers Magazine.* Mar. 2013: 29–37.

Niman, Michael. "6 Scary Extreme Energy Sources Being Tapped to Fuel the Post Peak Oil Economy." Seemorerocks Blog: Dirty Energy in the Post Peak Oil World. 15 Apr. 2012. <www.alternet.org/story/154936/6_scary_extreme_energy_sources_being_tapped_to_fuel_the_post_peak_oil_economy>

Shepard, Susan Elizabeth. "Wildcatting: A Stripper's Guide to the Modern American Boomtown." *Buzzfeed.* 13 July 2013. <www.buzzfeed.com/susanelizabethshepardwildcatting-a-strippers-guide-to-the-modern-american-boomtow>

Smith, Matt and Thom Patterson. "Debate over Fracking, Quakes Get Louder." CNN U.S.15 June 2012. <www.cnn.com/2012/06/15/us/fracking-earthquakes/index.html>

Switchboard: North Dakota Resources Defense Council Staff Blog. "A Suspected Cause of Drinking Water Contamination." 19 Dec. 2011. http://switchboard.nrdc.org/blogs/amall/incidents_where_ hydraulic_frac.html>

Walsh, Bryan. "The Truth About Oil." *Time* 9 Apr. 2012: 29–35.

ACKNOWLEDGMENTS

The author is grateful to the editors in the following journals in which the following poems originally appeared, sometimes in different forms:

Brevity	"Some Things About that Day"
Comstock Review	"Thugs" (published as "Invasive")
Georgetown Review	"Whisker Meditations"
The Ledge	"Never Mind" (published as "Cell") and "Greyhound Days"
Mississippi Review	"Nil Ductility"
Narrative Magazine	"Couples Traveling" and "Door-to-Door"
New Letters	"Lament"
The Normal School	"*Kablooey* Is the Sound You'll Hear"
North American Review	"To the Woman Who Tore the Word 'Husband' from the Oxford English Dictionary"
Oberon Review	"Bookmobile"
Opium	"Balance"
Rattle	"Buoy"
River Styx	"Lazer Land Outing with Boys," "Ground Oregano," and "Ecdysis"
RUNES: A Review of Poetry	"Chill Factor," from "Small Buried Things"
Southern Poetry Review	"Memorabilia" and "Scent"

A grouping of poems from this collection ("Things Not to Put in Your Mouth," "Poor You," "China: 5,000 Years," and "News Flash") were short-listed for the 2013 Manchester Poetry Prize, Manchester School of Writing, Manchester Metropolitan University, Manchester, UK.

Author's Note:
Many thanks to the art editors, the book team, and the publishing interns at

MSUM who worked on this book. I am grateful to the NRP staff, in particular the Co-Directors Alan R. Davis and Suzzanne Kelley, and especially to my editor, Thom Tammaro. Thank you for your patience and your belief in this book.

I'm also grateful to several additional writers who were associated with MSUM when I was a young, developing writer in the 1980s—Sally Herrin, Richard Zinober, David Mason, and Mark Vinz. May we all have the good fortune to be surrounded by a nurturing and inspiring community at the start of our writing lives.

ABOUT THE AUTHOR

Debra Marquart's books include two poetry collections—*Everything's a Verb* (New Rivers Press 1995) and *From Sweetness* (Pearl Editions 2002)—and a short story collection, *The Hunger Bone: Rock & Roll Stories* (New Rivers Press 2001), which draws on her experiences as a road musician. Marquart's work has received a Pushcart Prize, the Shelby Foote Nonfiction Prize from the Faulkner Society, the Headwaters Prize, and a National Endowment for the Arts Prose Fellowship. Marquart's memoir, *The Horizontal World: Growing Up Wild in the Middle of Nowhere* (Counterpoint Books 2006), was awarded the Elle Lettres Award from *Elle* Magazine and the 2007 PEN USA Creative Nonfiction Award. Marquart teaches in the Stonecoast Low-Residency MFA Program at University of Southern Maine, and she is a professor of English and the director of the MFA Program in Creative Writing and Environment at Iowa State University.

ABOUT NEW RIVERS PRESS

New Rivers Press emerged from a drafty Massachusetts barn in winter 1968. Intent on publishing work by new and emerging poets, founder C. W. "Bill" Truesdale labored for weeks over an old Chandler & Price letterpress to publish three hundred fifty copies of Margaret Randall's collection, *So Many Rooms Has a House But One Roof.*

Nearly four hundred titles later, New Rivers, a non-profit and now teaching press based since 2001 at Minnesota State University Moorhead, has remained true to Bill's goal to publish the best new literature—poetry and prose—from new and emerging writers in the Midwest. New Rivers Press has also broadened its mission through a series of innovative regional and national initiatives to offer encouragement, feedback, publication, and promotion to new, emerging, and established writers not only from the Midwest, but also from the culturally diverse national and international fraternity of writers.

Authors can be collaborators and partners at New Rivers. They range in age from twenty to eighty-nine. They include a silversmith, a carpenter, a geneticist, a monk, a tree-trimmer, and a rock musician. They hail from cities such as Christchurch, Honolulu, New Orleans, New York City, Northfield (Minnesota), and Prague.

Charles Baxter, one of the first authors with New Rivers, calls the press "the hidden backbone of the American literary tradition." Continuing this tradition, in 1981 New Rivers began to sponsor the Minnesota Voices Project (now called Many Voices Project) competition. It is one of the oldest literary competitions in the United States, bringing recognition and attention to emerging writers. Other New Rivers series publications include American Fiction Series, American Poetry Series, New Rivers Abroad, and the Electronic Book Series.